Your Family:
A Donor Kid's Story

Written by Wendy Kramer
Illustrated by Jen Moore

Your Family: A Donor Kid's Story
Copyright © 2018 the Donor Sibling Registry
and Wendy Kramer
Self-published

ALL RIGHTS RESERVED. No part of this book may be reproduced or transmitted in any form or by any means, electronic or mechanical, including photocopying, recording, or by an information storage and retrieval.

Introduction

There are only two lasting bequests we can hope to give our children. One is roots: the other wings.

• HODDING CARTER •

In 2000 my then ten year old donor-conceived son Ryan and I started the Donor Sibling Registry (DSR). It was born out of his curiosity about possible half siblings and about his own biological father, a man only known to us as donor 1058. From the beginning, the DSR's mission has been to connect, educate and support all those in the donor family, first and foremost being the donor-conceived children.

18 years later, with 60,000 members in 105 countries, and with many research studies and published papers, we've come to understand much about everyone in the donor family. With almost 20,000 people connected on the DSR, we've heard from thousands of them about the profound and important familial connections that take place every single day. We know that it's important for donor offspring to be told about their origins right from the start - but telling is only the first step. Donor-conceived children must also feel understood about their own curiosities and eagerness to connect with their first and second-degree genetic relatives, and their desire to know more about their ancestry. To quote Bruce Springsteen, "You can't really know who you are, and where you're going unless you know where you came from."

Over the years, I have been asked many times to recommend a children's book about being donor-conceived, being curious about half siblings and donors, and about making those connections. Here it is! I have tried in this book to be sensitive to everyone in the donor family. Because terminology is a hot button, I use several terms to describe both half siblings (donor siblings) and biological parents (donors). I believe that parents should be as accurate as possible with the terminology, knowing that most kids, at some point, will want to try on all the terms. Terminology will likely change over the years, with maturity and the ability to define these relationships for themselves. I encourage all parents to think deeply and critically about the terminology so that all donor kids feel supported and free to use any of and all of the words that they need to as they grow up. Because there are an infinite number of combinations of family type, parent type, donor type, sibling type and child type, we show many types of kids and families in the book. After reading each page, parents can springboard into conversations with their child about how their own family is unique and special.

Children may go through many phases and levels of curiosity. Some may be mildly curious, some not at all, and some have a burning desire to know their first and second-degree genetic relatives. Parents need to be ready to support and honor any curiosities that their child might have as they mature.

My hope is that this book will be a great tool for opening up conversations between parents and young children with the goal, as always, to create happy and healthy donor families.

Wendy Kramer

Praise for Your Family: A Donor Kid's Story

*"**Your Family: A Donor Kid's Story** is a wonderful book that affirms the experience of children who have been donor-conceived. It's important for families to have a book like this to read to their kids, so that their children can understand who they are and where they came from. Wendy Kramer's book is long overdue!"*

- Jacqueline Mroz, author of *Scattered Seeds: In Search of Family and Identity in the Sperm Donor Generation*

"As a psychotherapist, I work with many LGBT parents of donor conceived children who struggle to find the right language to speak to their children about the circumstance of their birth. They are also often afraid that learning about their donors and potential donor siblings will be upsetting or confusing to their children. Finally, I have a book to recommend to them! ***Your Family: A Donor Kid's Story*** is the perfect combination of honest, loving, and positive. I am keeping a pile of copies in my office."

- Liz Margolies, LCSW, psychotherapist and mother of a donor-conceived child

"***Your Family: A Donor Kid's Story*** gives children born from egg or sperm donation a chance to see themselves reflected in a positive, informative and accessible story. Most importantly, this book will help families who have used reproductive technology to explain complex concepts to their children while giving them vital information about themselves and how they came to be. Here's a book that is relatable and will allow children to feel proud of their special story."

- Susan Frankel, MFT, licensed marriage and family therapist and mother to a donor-conceived daughter

"As the proud Grandmother of a donor child, I am so pleased to see this wonderful book! I think it will help donor children understand just how special and loved they are. ***Your Family: A Donor Kid's Story*** allows parents to ease into giving the child the information they need for a complete life and for understanding how different families can look."

- Jacki K, grandmother

"Thank you to Wendy and Ryan for all of their dedication and hard work bringing more openness, acceptance and connection of donor-conceived people and families. As a donor-conceived person, I had such a strong need to know my biological roots and family. I would have greatly benefited from being able to talk about being a donor-conceived person at a young age. Thank you for this wonderful book to help parents talk about this aspect of their child's life with them. Children need to know that who they are is accepted and comfortable for their parents, and that they are able to talk about their life, no matter how they were created."

- **Lynne W. Spencer, RN, MA, author of *Sperm Donor Offspring; Identity and Other Experiences***

"Wow! I wish I'd had this book when I was growing up. It would have explained everything. It should be given to every donor kid."

- **B. Richard, donor-conceived college student**

"A creative and comfortable way to talk to our donor-conceived kids about their origins."

- **Ann Dixon, Co-founder, Serendip Studio**

"This easy-to-read, attractively illustrated book ought to be distributed to donor-conceived children and their parents as standard practice. It introduces to young children what it means to be donor-conceived, helps their parents broach an often awkward subject, and will help obviate any stigma surrounding children's origins. Such a little book could have made a major difference in my life growing up."

- **Albert Frantz, donor-conceived adult**

"Cool book. Pretty sure it's the first book I ever got to read about donor siblings. It's good that someone's writing about kids with donor siblings because a lot of us have them. Kids without donor siblings should read this book too, because I get tired of having to explain my family to people. My favorite part of the book was when I got to write down questions I have for my donor. That was pretty cool. I hope a lot of people read this book."

- **Gabrielle Capasso, Age 11**

"While I wish this book had been available back when my daughter was little and I desperately needed it, I'm thrilled to know that parents of donor kids now have a book that describes their family. I think **Your Family: A Donor Kid's Story**, will prove to be an invaluable tool—providing an inclusive, age appropriate way to celebrate each child's story and describe what makes their family so special. Thank you for creating such a beautiful story, it's been a long time coming. I highly recommend this book!"

- **Meredyth Capasso, mom to 11 year old Gabi**

"Having worked with Wendy Kramer for many years I know her organization Donor Sibling Registry (DSR) is valuable to the LGBTQ parenting community. We've published family stories that talk about how DSR has brought joy to not just the half siblings discovering each other but to their gay parents as well. Kramer's children's book **Your Family: A Donor Kid's Story** is an important contribution to the LGBTQ community and a great addition to the homes of all parents with donor-conceived children."

- **Angeline Acain, publisher and editor, Gay Parent Magazine**

"What a beautiful way to help donor children make sense of their stories! Wendy Kramer's open-hearted new book sees the love in families of all kinds and honors kids' curiosity about their genetic connections. This book will help donor children recognize themselves—it acknowledges that their families are real and worth getting to know, in all their possibilities. I wish I'd had this book when I was young…"

- **Sara Lamm, documentary filmmaker and donor-conceived person**

"As a psychologist, I hear from parents who are frustrated with the lack of children-focused books on donor-conceived children's feelings and questions. Wendy's book encourages family discussions about the special opportunity of donor-sibling relationships. I'm looking forward to using her book both professionally and personally."

- **Debbie Ramirez, Ph.D., mother to two egg donor-conceived children**

Dedicated to Ryan Kramer

...and all the kids who were
born out of love.

You were born just like every other kid in the world, from a tiny sperm cell and a tiny egg cell.

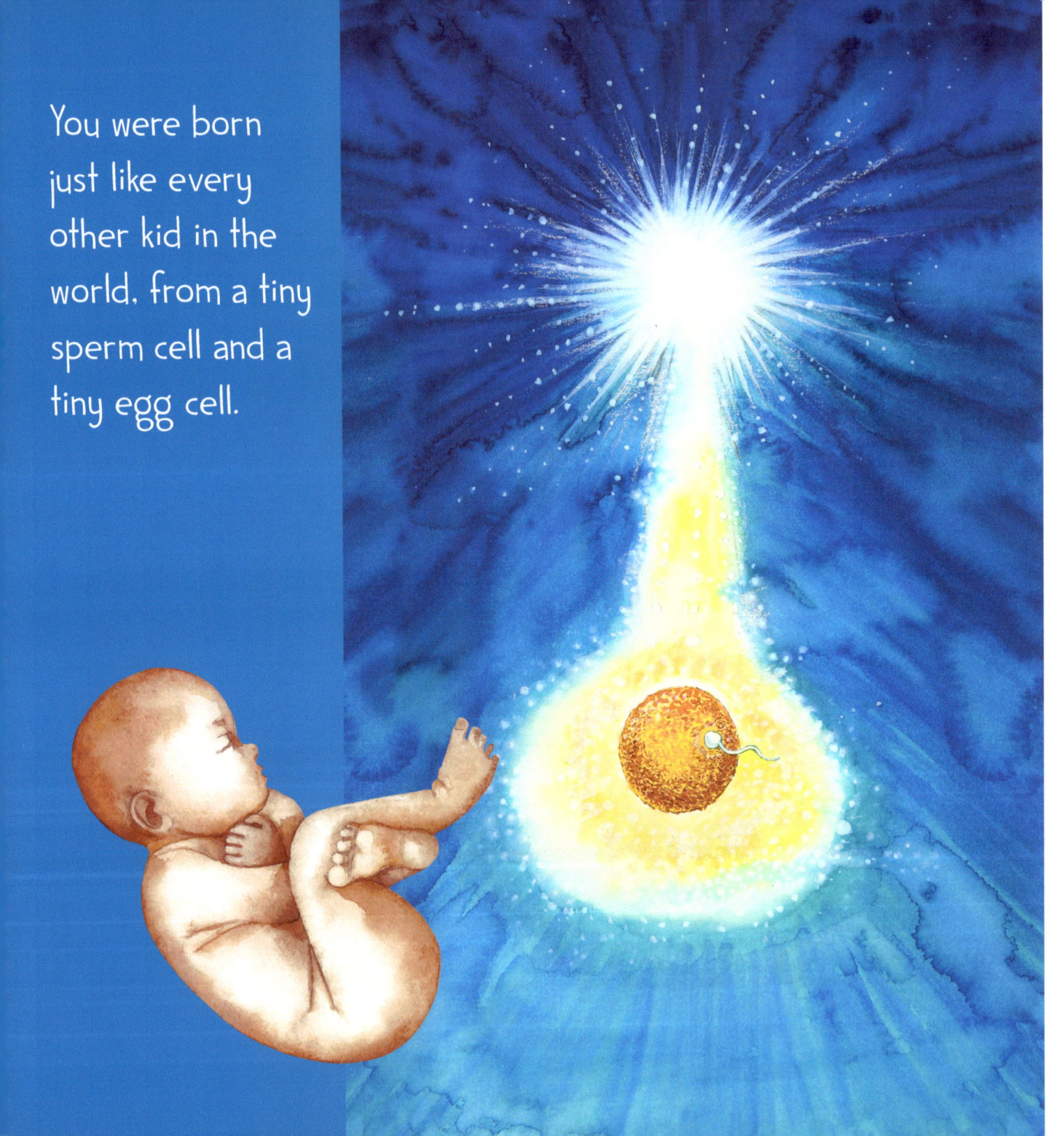

You were born out of love.

A long time ago, your parent(s) wished for a baby.

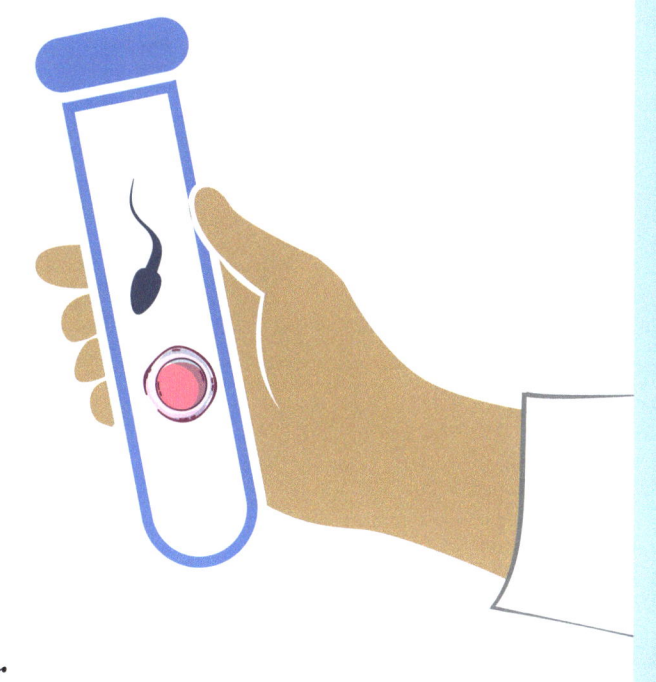

Because it takes both a sperm cell and an egg cell to make a baby, your parents went to a clinic for the missing cell they needed to create you.

The person who gave the sperm or egg cell to the clinic is sometimes called the donor, a person who helps parents like yours have the children they've always dreamed of having.

DONOR
BROWN EYES
BROWN HAIR
5'9"
LIKES DOGS

A donor is a special type of biological parent who is different from the parents who raise you and take care of you.

When the egg and sperm first joined together, that was the very beginning of you!

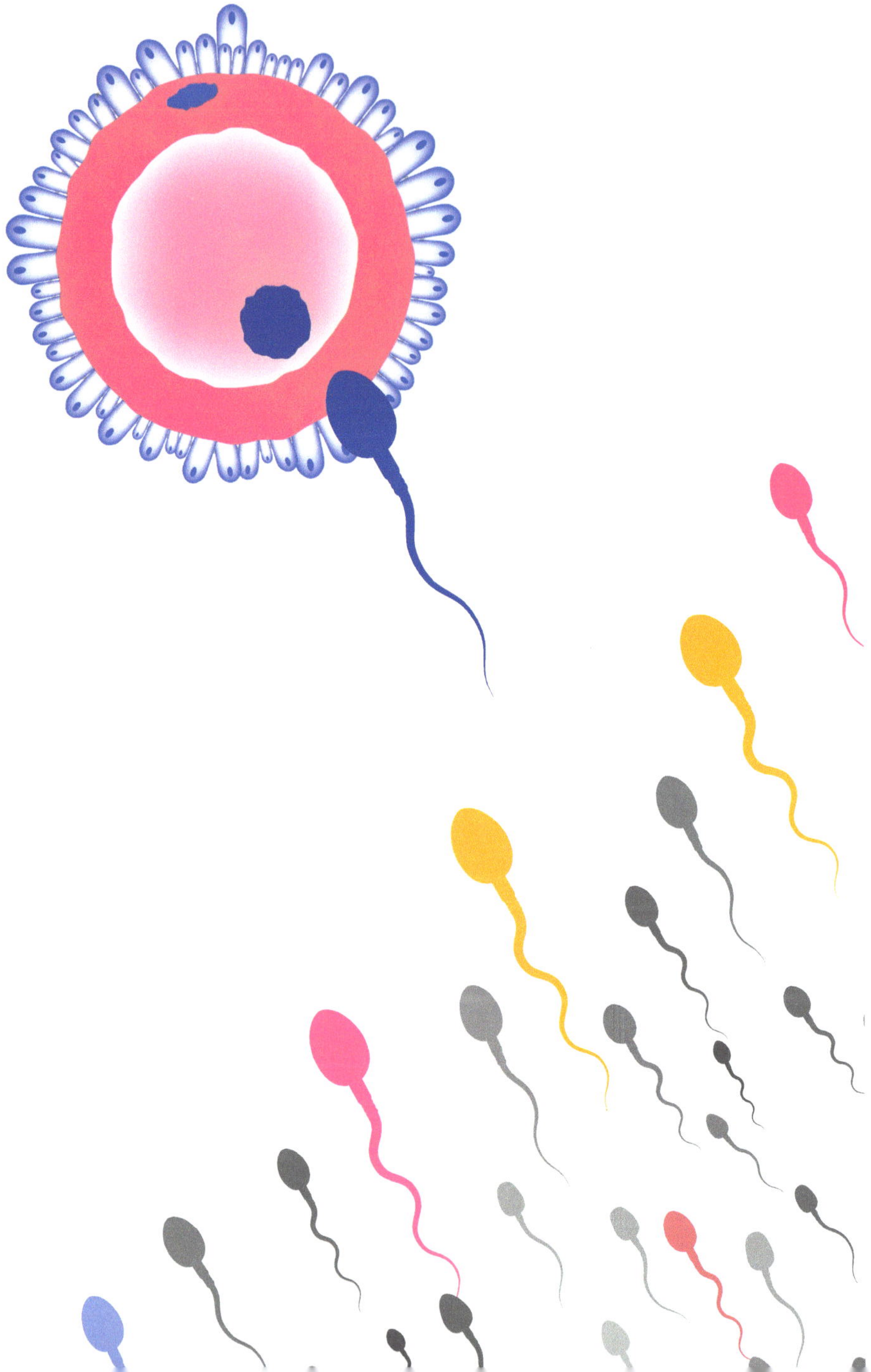

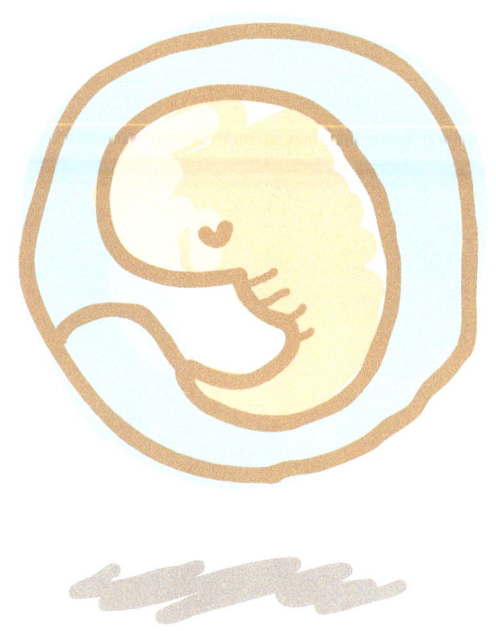

GLUE A GRAIN OF RICE HERE
TO SEE HOW SMALL
YOU WERE AT ONE MONTH

You were so tiny at first, no bigger than the tiniest freckle. After a month you were only the size of a single grain of rice.

After 9 months, you arrived into the world as a perfect and beautiful baby. Your whole family celebrated!

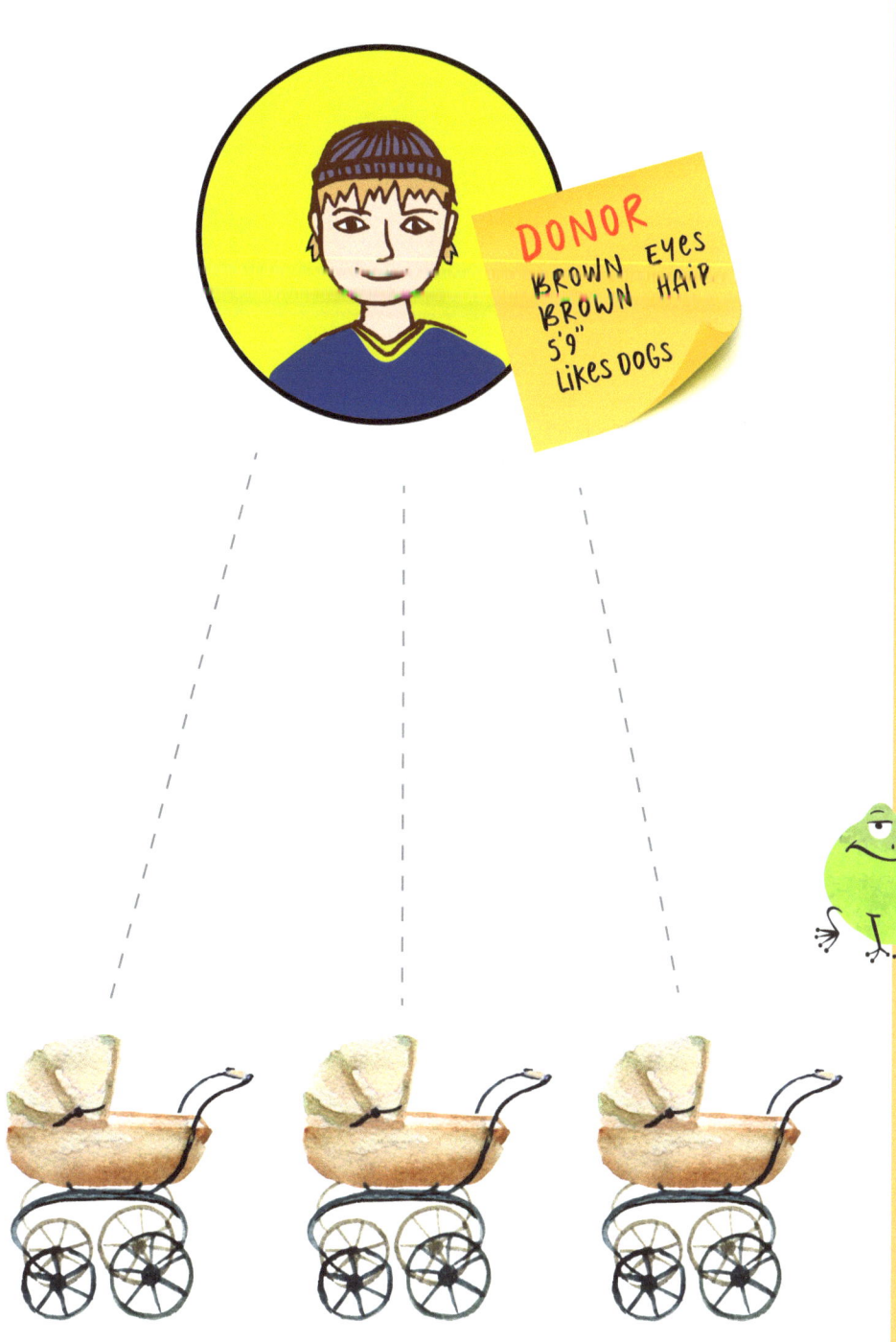

Because there were other families who also needed to use a donor to have a baby, some of them used the very same donor.

That means that there are other kids like you! Because all those families used the same donor to create their children, it means that those kids are your half siblings. They can also be called your donor siblings, or your half brothers and half sisters.

HENRY

SHELLY

BIANCA

RYAN

GRACIE

JAI

2 MOMS

2 DADS

SINGLE MOM

MOM & DAD

SINGLE DAD

There are many types of families. Some of your half siblings might have one mom or dad, or two moms, or a mom and a dad, or two dads.

All families are connected by love, and some are also connected through biology. How about your family? Do you have brothers or sisters that you are growing up with?

WHAT'S YOUR SIBLING STORY?

Some kids really want to meet their donor siblings, and even the person who gave the sperm or egg, as they all share very special parts of themselves.

Maybe they share a love for dogs, or playing piano, or being good at soccer, or beautiful brown eyes, or loving math, or even their funny ears. Half siblings can share so many special and unique things with each other.

DOES ANYBODY LIKE BUGS?

BROWN EYES

What things do you think you share with your donor or your half brothers and sisters?

FUNNY EARS

$$\begin{array}{r}37\\ \times\ 37\\ \hline 1369\end{array}$$

WHAT DO YOU THINK YOU SHARE?

Some kids are very curious and some only just a little. How about you? Would you like to send them a letter? Talk on the phone? See a picture? Would you like to meet your donor or half siblings one day?

DSR   MESSAGE
eMAIL
PHOTO   PHONE
LETTER

If your donor siblings live nearby, you might get to see them all the time. But sometimes they live far away, so getting together can be a very special occasion.

You can meet at your home, or at the park, or at the beach, or even plan a party!

LIST OF PLACES:

_____

_____

_____

_____

_____

Where would you like to meet your half siblings?

Your donor might have a family of their own. And guess what? Your donor's kids are also your half siblings.

You might have one or two or maybe even a whole lot of half siblings out there. How do you feel about that?

What would you like your half siblings and donor to know about you?

ABOUT ME

FAVORITE TV SHOW OR MOVIE

FAVORITE HOBBY

PHOTO OF ME

MY PET

THINGS I'M GOOD AT ....

FAVORITE MUSIC ....

FAVORITE ANIMALS ....

SPORTS I PLAY ....

MY BEST FRIEND ....

Here is a page for your half brothers and sisters.

MY HALF BROTHERS AND SISTERS

I HAVE ☐   HAVE NOT ☐ MET THEM

I'D LIKE TO KNOW:

PHOTO

PHOTO

What fun things have you already done, or would you like to do with your half siblings?

WE WENT TO ....

WE WANT TO GO TO ....

PLANS WE WILL MAKE ....

....

THEIR NAMES ....

DRAW WHAT YOU THINK YOUR DONOR LOOKS LIKE

```
┌ ─ ─ ─ ─ ─ ─ ─ ─ ─ ─ ─ ─ ┐
│                         │
│                         │
│                         │
│                         │
│                         │
└ ─ ─ ─ ─ ─ ─ ─ ─ ─ ─ ─ ─ ┘
```

MY DONOR:

DONOR NUMBER ....

SPERM BANK OR EGG CLINIC

....

NAME ....

You can list everything that you know about the donor and all the things you're curious to know about.

Here is a page for you and your family.

I LOVE MY FAMILY BECAUSE:

....

....

....

ABOUT MY FAMILY

BROTHERS ....

SISTERS ....

WHAT I CALL MY PARENT(S)

....

....

PHOTOS AND DRAWINGS OF MY FAMILY

The Donor Sibling Registry
EDUCATING, CONNECTING AND SUPPORTING DONOR FAMILIES

**Your Family: A Donor Kid's Story Is Sponsored by
The Donor Sibling Registry: Educating, Connecting, and Supporting Donor Families**

The Donor Sibling Registry (DSR) was founded in 2000 to assist individuals conceived as a result of sperm, egg, or embryo donation who are seeking to make mutually desired contact with others with whom they share genetic ties. Without any outside support, the DSR has pioneered an international discussion about the donor conception industry and the families, with its research, media appearances, speaking engagements, and interviews. The DSR advocates for the right to honesty and transparency for donor-conceived people, for social acceptance and legal rights, and values the diversity of all families. The DSR's core value is honesty, with the conviction that people have the fundamental right to information about their biological origins and identities.

Parents are sometimes not prepared for their children's curiosity and desire to know more about their genetic background. In order to move out of the secrecy and shame that has for so long shrouded donor conception, the DSR will continue to educate parents and the general public on the importance of honoring and supporting their children's natural drive to know more about their identity. The DSR also ensures that the donor-conceived have a safe place to search for their biological identities and to make these connections with their half siblings and where possible, their donors as well.

Finding Our Families: A First-of-Its-Kind Book for Donor-Conceived People and Their Families

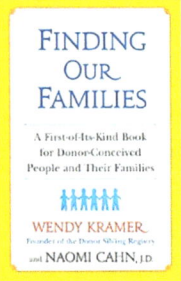

Millions of people have been born with the help of donor sperm or eggs, including Wendy Kramer's son. Realizing the unique concerns of being or parenting a donor-conceived child, Kramer launched what would become the world's largest database for connecting donor-conceived people, the Donor Sibling Registry (DSR). ***Finding Our Families*** provides additional support for this growing community. With compassion and insight, the authors draw on extensive research to address situations families face throughout a donor-conceived child's development, including the search for a biological parent or half sibling, and how to forge a healthy self-image.

"The book successfully honors its promise to deliver the tools necessary to help donor-conceived children discover and explore their genetic legacies."

- 10/13 Publisher's Weekly review

www.ingramcontent.com/pod-product-compliance
Lightning Source LLC
Chambersburg PA
CBHW042142290426
44110CB00002B/86